TEACHING
BRITISH
VALUES
TO CHILDREN

Teaching British Values to Children

Published by Deborah Osborne

Copyright © 2016 by Deborah Osborne

The right of Deborah Osborne to be identified as the author of this work has been asserted by them in accordance with the Copyright, Designs and Patents Act 1988.

ISBN: 978-1-5262-0130-0

Book design by *www.wordzworth.com*

TEACHING
BRITISH
VALUES
TO CHILDREN

Ideas for games, activities and so much more to
support you in teaching the British values principles

DEBORAH OSBORNE

"What are we without confidence, self-belief and hope" ...

N<small>O, IT'S NOT A</small> 'S<small>TEVE</small> J<small>OBS</small>' <small>QUOTE</small>

A bit about me.

I have been working in Early Years' childcare and education intermittently for thirty years. My current role is in a full day nursery setting where I am the preschool room manager, EYFS co-ordinator, safeguarding officer, SENco and third in charge. I have been fortunate enough to receive some excellent training over the years, particularly in speech and language development. I have used this experience to provide in house training for staff to support children's development in this area. I would say my passion is building children's confidence and self-esteem: I believe it's the key to future success – that and a sense of humour. I would add that I feel that, as adults, we have a responsibility to speak positively to children, particularly about this country. My hope is that it will inspire them to feel more optimistic about their future prospects, giving them more enthusiasm and incentives to work hard in school.

I have written from my experience as a 'hands on' practitioner. My moto is "don't ask anyone to do something you're not prepared to do yourself", so I am personally implementing these ideas and activities in my current setting.

Thank you for your interest.

Please feel free to email me for more information.

Deborah

debsosborne@live.co.uk

CONTENTS

INTRODUCTION:
WHY TEACH 'BRITISH VALUES'?

Safe guarding our children and the country's security

In light of the concerns over the possible radicalization of children, the British Government has introduced a new 'Prevent Duty' law. This law includes teaching 'British values' in early years and school settings. The teaching of the four values and principles of:

- Democracy

- The Rule of Law

- Individual Liberty and Freedom for All

- Mutual Respect and Tolerance of those with Different Faiths and Beliefs

are now a curriculum requirement.

The Department for Education has issued some guidance notes relating to how teachers and child care professionals can implement this policy. However, from conducting online research and speaking directly to those in the teaching profession, the consensus I draw is that practitioners would appreciate tangible methods and ideas to support them in teaching this subject. There have been references indicating that childcare settings could be at risk of losing their funding if they cannot show Ofsted inspectors that they are implementing this new legislation.

The Department of Education has advised that displaying posters and having the odd cultural artefact or book with subliminal messages will not be sufficient evidence to show Ofsted that children are being taught these values. As a consequence, schools and nurseries could face having their Ofsted rating downgraded. So how **can** you 'prove it'?

How this book can support you

This book has been written specifically to enable teachers and childcare professionals to expand on the existing strategies used to encourage children's personal, social, moral and spiritual development and to implement new strategies for teaching the British values. It is formatted into four chapters. Each chapter focuses on one of the four 'British values' and its principles. There is an overview of the EYFS prime and specific areas of learning with examples of how the key principles are already imbedded in the curricula for early years' education and for schools. I have used classroom scenarios and Q&As to model the type of vocabulary that you can use daily to develop children's understanding of this subject. In addition to this, there are games, activities, suggested topics, songs, rhymes and specific reading matter to support you in providing concrete evidence that you are actively teaching this subject. The tone and ethos is very positive, promoting and teaching the key principles of the new policy in a fun, educational, thought-provoking way.

The concept can be adapted to suit different age ranges by using more or less complex vocabulary and questions as appropriate. Incorporated are a variety of non-verbal gestures for children to use, for example raising their hands or putting their thumbs up or down to indicate whether they think something is good or not good etc. The aim is to promote an ethos of inclusivity by encouraging those children with low self-confidence, SEND, EAL and/or delayed speech and language development to participate in the discussions. This book is not political. The content aims to provide a bit of support and inspiration ... I hope you find the ideas useful.

How the British values are already embedded into the curriculum

The "British values" key principles and promotion of children's spiritual, moral, social, cultural and physical development are already embedded in the early years and schools' curricula. The 'values' and 'principles' are not defined to a particular area of learning: they merge, enabling teachers and early years' professionals to plan lessons and link elements of S.M.S.C.P development and the 'values' into most subjects. Developing a really good understanding of this subject and the ethos behind why it has been introduced into the curriculum is arguably key to how enthusiastic educators will be about adding new ideas and concepts into their teaching. My understanding of the "Prevent Duty" law and the purpose behind promoting the 'values' is that by combining the governments new strategies with existing ones and teaching them holistically, hopefully children will be more aware, less vulnerable and even more equipped to achieve the "Every child matters outcomes".

Listed in this introductory chapter are some examples of how to merge the values into the EYFS 'prime' and 'specific' areas of learning. Primary schools are achieving this through lessons in, for example, citizenship, personal, social, health and religious education. Furthermore, it gives suggestions of how you can expand on your learning intentions by linking them to other subjects, for example, mathematics, literacy, communication and language development.

The examples given are not exhaustive and are open to interpretation. For further clarity on this subject please refer to the early years "Development matters characteristics of effective learning" or "National curriculum hand book" for primary school teachers, key stage 1 and 2.

In the Three Prime Areas

Personal, Social and Emotional Development – the Rule of Law

The main learning intentions for this area are to develop children's self-confidence, individuality and self-belief. It focuses on supporting children in being able to manage their feelings and behaviour. Give children praise and encourage them to verbalise their emotions, preferences and to discuss their experiences. Instil an understanding and respect for the law. Explain how rules and boundaries apply to them and are put in place to keep them safe. Promote good practise in relation to manners – for example, how children speak to each other and or having good table manners etc. Develop a deeper understanding of the importance of sharing, turn taking, friendship, consideration, tolerance and respect. Support children in developing an appreciation and gratitude for the opportunities that are afforded them, particularly through education and the advantages of living in this country.

Unique Child	Confidence
Role models	Self-esteem
Education	Negotiation
Friendship	Self-respect
Nurturing relationships	Kindness
Positive relationships	Morality
Rules	Socialising
Boundaries	Giving
Affection	Sharing
Respect	Economic wellbeing
Tolerance	Receiving
Consideration	Health
Care	Manners

Communication and Language Development – Prevent Duty Law

The main learning intentions for this area are to develop children's speech, language, communication, attention, listening and understanding. Promoting confidence, clear speech, a wide vocabulary and good communication skills is a key to enabling children to safeguard themselves in society. We need children to develop their expressive language to enable them to verbalise their thoughts, feelings and experiences. You can link this to the 'prevent duty' law as often we learn more about a child's home life and possible safeguarding issues etc, through 'comments' they might make during conversation and or play. Develop an ethos of tolerance and respect for others by encouraging the children to listen to each other's viewpoints, preferences and opinions. Set boundaries for listening to others and not interrupting when someone else is speaking. Praise them for their resilience in contributing to discussions and model language particularly to support those with delayed speech, EAL or SEN. Encourage children to feel confident to speak in a one to one or group situation, allow them time to process their thoughts and transfer them into words. Give recognition and show appreciation for what has been said. Instil an understanding of the children's rights to express their opinions and viewpoints and an appreciation of how powerful words can be.

Safeguarding	Disclosure
Critical thinking	Influence
Freedom of speech	Expressive language
Communication	Confidence
Conversation	Self-esteem
Respect for others	Individual power
Opinions	Courage
Viewpoints	Collective power
Vocabulary	Opportunity
Preferences	Influence
Tolerance	Responsibility

Physical development – Individual Liberty and Freedom for All

The main learning intentions for this area are to develop children's fine and gross motor skills. Furthermore, it aims to build their awareness of healthy eating practises and the importance of exercise for a healthy mind and body. Praise and encourage children to be independent, develop their self-help skills e.g. dressing/ undressing, pouring their own drinks etc and personal hygiene skills e.g. toileting and handwashing. If they say "I can't do it" then we need to encourage them to try and to not 'give up' which shows your building their resilience. You can support children's development in this area by Introducing fun, challenging games and activities. Give opportunities for the children to make choices, for example self-selecting activities and resources. Allow them to explore their environment, get messy, and to take supervised risks to further develop their abilities and self-esteem. Focus on sportsmanship, working individually and as part of a team. Develop an appreciation of the right to be able to try new things. Explain that they are fortunate to be able to learn and develop new skills within safe boundaries. Promote an ethos of inclusivity and equality, giving opportunities for all children to join in. You can refer to the 'rule of law' when introducing games with specific rules for example no cheating or introduce a democratic process for choosing games and activities. Examples of this are given in the chapter on democracy.

Enabling environments	Resilience
Developing new skills	Challenges
Developing independence	Tolerance
Control	Choice
Active learning	Exercise
Strength of character	Learning
Sportsmanship	Exploring
Advancement	Obstacles

Perseverance

Encouragement

Patience

Sharing

Aspirations

Success

Achievement

Equality

Health

Self respect

In the Four Specific Areas

Literacy Development – Individual Liberty and Freedom for All – Heritage

The main learning intentions for this area are to develop children's reading and writing skills. This can be challenging for many children, so build their resilience, give praise, make it fun and interesting. Expand on their learning by explaining that many songs, rhymes and stories etc date back centuries. Have fun with phonics activities: be creative and bring stories and words to life by using props, expressive language and an enthusiastic tone. Instil an appreciation and respect of books, poetry and rhymes. Explain how reading and writing can help them to reach their goals. Explain that this is another platform to voice their opinions and viewpoints etc. Give children an understanding that the written word is an influential media. You could merge the "rule of law" and "mutual respect and tolerance of those with different faiths and beliefs" by discussing that words need to be used carefully, give examples of how the written word reinforces laws, and can potentially affect a person's happiness and or hurt others. This would be particularly relevant in regards to social media e.g. cyber bullying etc.

Education	Reading
Writing	Books
Self-expression	Poetry
Exploring	Research
Learning	Experience
Opportunity	Languages
Self-development	Self-esteem
Knowledge	Respect
Tolerance	Power
Boundaries	Influence
Resilience	Legislation
Vocabulary	Achievement
Responsibility	Consideration

Mathematics – All Four Values

The main learning intentions for this area are to develop children's understanding of numbers, shape, space and measure. Mathematics in relation to money, the economy and how money is earned, used and perceived affects us socially and morally. Finances impact on family, economic well-being, leisure time, health and so on. By listing these examples, it reinforces how you can merge social, moral, economic development and aspects of the the British values principles into most if not all subjects. Take for example "tolerance", you can link this to people having to be tolerant of working conditions, government cut backs etc. "Rule of law" this is an easy one, honesty and having to pay for things etc. Arguably, children should develop an understanding of money, you could introduce this subject in organised role play activities, by discussing pocket money and or why parents work and so on. There are moral lessons to be learned, however earning money is essential. Perhaps the lesson to teach children is that persevering and achieving in education is realistically their best chance of reaching their economic and lifestyle goals.

Economic wellbeing	Security
Population	Opportunity
Percentages	Earnings
Counting	Honesty
Migration	Health
Currency	Responsibility
Occupation	Tolerance
Industry	Receiving
Wealth	Greed
Poverty	Corruption
Rules and regulations	Influence
Contribution	Resilience
Power	Perseverance
Philanthropy	Charity

Understanding the World – All Four Values

The main learning intentions for this area are to develop children's understanding and awareness of people, communities, the world as a whole and technology. The British values are a set of values to safeguard our children. The phrase "teaching British values" has caused concern and even offence to some people. However, the British values principles are arguably about common decency, respect and tolerance applied to all areas of a person's life. It's about having an attitude of gratitude and loyalty to a country that offers its occupants so much freedom and opportunity. There is currently a lot of negative emphasis in relation to religion and religious beliefs, however, generally speaking, children rarely if ever spontaneously refer to religion. The "Understanding the World" area covers a broad spectrum, making it arguably the most influential area of learning. This is reflected in the key words listed below. There are a multitude of brilliant learning opportunities within this area, not least because all the values merge easily in to it. When planning, particularly for topics, document your learning intentions in relation to teaching the 'values'. This should provide you with some good supporting evidence to show you are actively teaching them to the children. Suggestions for topics and examples of how you can merge the values into them, are given in the 'additional resources' chapter.

People

Preferences

Communities

Diversity

Occupations

Families

Similarities and differences

Experiences

Faiths

Beliefs

History

Heritage

Geography

Laws

Cultural experiences

Celebrations

Economic education	Traditions
Aspirations	Recreational pastimes
Food	Opportunity
Holidays	Influence
Countries	Power
Environment	Sharing
Languages	Giving
Diversity	Resilience
Technology	Character

Expressive Art and Design – All Four Values

The main learning intentions for this area are to develop children's creativity through expressive art, design and different forms of media – for example, music and dance. Gender stereo types can be broken down, particularly for young children when they are exploring roleplay. They have opportunities to express their feelings, ideas and viewpoints through creative play. Children tend to deviate towards the home corner: it is very often the hub where they do most of their social interaction, talking and negotiation. They appear unaware that they themselves develop their own democratic processes and rules. Children will reprimand each other, setting boundaries within their play. Frequently, they collectively decide how a game should be organised, who the key players are and what the plot is. There are the dominant characters who usually get the lead roles – for example, Mum, Dad or the big sister. You can guarantee someone is going to get upset because they want to be the 'princess' not a 'baby' or the 'dog' – it's so interesting! There are instances where cultural beliefs and view points can conflict with a child's rights to explore all forms of expressive art and design. Examples of this can be parents not wanting their child to get messy or not wanting their son to wear the princess dress etc. Fortunately, though, it is generally accepted that these forms of expression are a natural part of a child's freedom to explore the environment. Playing collectively, dressing up, mimicking what they have observed at home, exploring cultural artefacts and so on is a subtle introduction to understanding cultural diversity. Play-based learning develops children's understanding of similarities and difference that connect them and/or make them unique while developing an ethos of individuality, tolerance and appreciation of an individual's right to freedom of expression. The early years' foundation stage curriculum is based around learning through play. The children are engaged in learning because they are generally uninhibited to really be their authentic self, exploring, being creative, challenged, challenging, making choices and … having fun!

Friendship

Playing

Exploring

Self-expression

Media

Democracy

Music/Dance

Cultural role play

Dressing up

Religious festivals

Cultural displays

Confidence

Rules

Appreciation

Respect

Boundaries

Self-esteem

Experimenting

Equality of opportunity

Interaction

Cultural artefacts

Choice

Cooperation

Gender equality

Freedom

Character

Tolerance

Acceptance

Freedom of expression

Authenticity

1

DEMOCRACY

Democracy

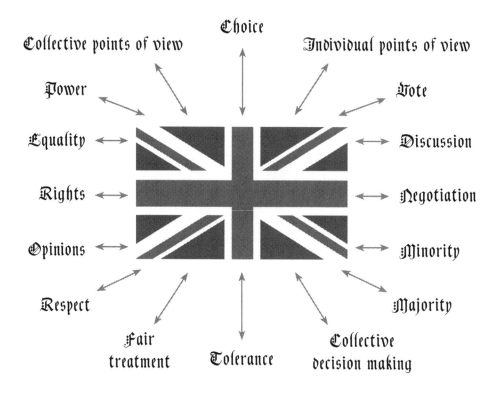

This section focuses on compromise, negotiation, equality and the implementation of a fair democratic process in the classroom through discussion. As the children develop more of an understanding of what democracy means, you can introduce the words "vote", "equality" and "tolerance". Children should be encouraged to join in discussions and to raise their hands to reinforce their views and opinions, for example by the showing of hands in the form of a vote for a particular activity. You could prepare for the introduction of this subject by making ballot boxes and voting cards – how to make and implement the ballot boxes is featured in this chapter. Use them as visual aids to support your explanation of the democratic process and to make it fun. Here is a scenario of how the concept of democracy can be introduced as a defined subject matter. The vocabulary is fairly basic. It is for teachers to judge the introduction of more complex vocabulary and expand on sentence structure in line with children's stages of development.

Teacher speaks to pupils

" *We are going to be learning about a big, important word today. The word is democracy. Let us say it together ... DEMOCRACY. Let's talk about this word and what it means. Democracy is when we come together as a group. You are all sitting on the carpet together. That means you are a group of children. As a group, we can talk about all the different things that we might want to do or things we might want to change. We all sit together and listen to each other's ideas. This is so we make sure we are being fair to everyone in the class. Democracy is about all of us being treated as equals. Equals means no one is better than anyone else. You are all special and what you think is **very, very** important.*

Let's look at ways we have democracy or fairness in our classroom and school. "

Through discussion, you can make a list of the democratic process in the classroom. If your classroom doesn't have one, then you could implement some of the suggestions in this chapter.

    " *It is very important to talk to each other about what we think are good ideas.* "

If you have any special events coming up – for example Christmas, summer fête etc. – you can ask the children to input their ideas. Alternatively, suggest something you could change in the classroom so you have real examples of a democratic process that produces results.

    " *Let us look at how you use your ideas when you are playing, how do you let your friends know what you want or what you are thinking?* "

You can supplement with examples, such as "please can I have a turn" or "I don't want to play that game".

    " *The biggest way you let your friends know what your ideas are and what you want is by talking to each other. It's very important to use your words when you play with your friends and when you're speaking to grown-ups. If you use your words, then we know what you're thinking, and how you feel about something.* "

This next scenario works well if you have made the ballot boxes and voting cards, but if you have not made them yet, you can improvise with a show of hands.

    " *What would you like to have out on the carpet today? Let's take a vote. If you want stickle bricks, put your voting card in the blue box. If you want magnets, put your vote in the red box. Let's count the votes.* "

You can then count up the votes, explain which activity got the most votes and therefore, that activity will go on the carpet. Explain that they have just made a democratic decision. Make it fair for the minority by negotiating a time when they can have the activity that lost the vote.

" *Children, I am so proud of you. You showed me you were listening, and did good talking and joining in … Give yourselves a clap.* "

Activity – Making ballot boxes and voting cards

This activity is key to implementing the democratic process in your classroom and will be needed to support other activities in this book.

One of the key strategies to develop children's understanding of democracy is allowing them to vote. To do that, we are going to need two ballot boxes and enough voting cards for all the children in the room. Using two simple, visual choices is an easy way to introduce the idea of voting.

STEP ONE

Make it fun! Involve the children by encouraging them to paint each box individually in a different colour – for example one red, one blue.

STEP TWO

If you have the time and the resources (yes I do have a sense of humour), take small individual pictures of the children and stick them onto individual pieces of card. Encourage them to write or 'mark make' their names on the back, laminate them so they last longer. Alternatively, use card that they can write their names on the back of and laminate them.

Now you're ready to implement the voting process in the class.

Scenario

66 *What shall we have out on the carpet today? Let's take a vote. Put your picture (voting card) in the red box if you want the Lego. Put it in the blue box if you want the cars.* 99

Encourage the children to count up the votes. Explain that, by voting, they have made a democratic decision. Give the group with the least amount of votes an opportunity to access the activity at an alternative time or, if convenient, in a different area.

Activity – Let me see a show of hands

One of the activities in the chapter on "Mutual respect and Tolerance" is hand printing. Here is an activity using these hand prints that will help to support your democratic process. You can link this activity to literacy development.

STEP ONE

Laminate the hand prints after the children have "mark made" or written their name on the back.

STEP TWO

Attach them to a straw or lolly stick.

You're set to go ... Let the children hold them up, use them to vote, reinforce their views, opinions and generally have fun with them. It is also a great tool for children with delayed speech and language development etc to encourage them to join in, particularly during circle time discussions.

2

RULE OF LAW

Rule of Law

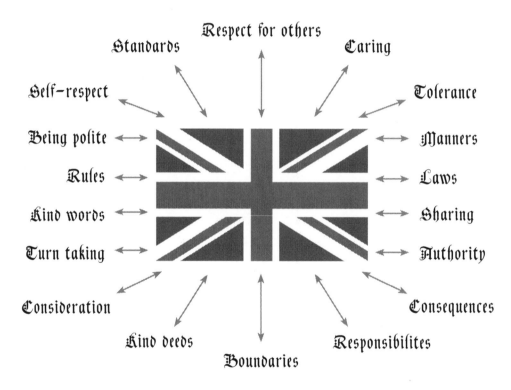

Respect for others

Standards

Caring

Self-respect

Tolerance

Being polite

Manners

Rules

Laws

Kind words

Sharing

Turn taking

Authority

Consideration

Consequences

Kind deeds

Responsibilites

Boundaries

This section focuses on boundaries, respect for others, being kind and considerate, tolerance, consequences, manners (including table manners), social expectations and respect for people in authority. It encourages the children to develop an understanding of the link between school rules and those in society. Children should be encouraged to put their thumbs up or down to support their opinions. Every opportunity should be utilised to build the children's confidence, self-esteem and to make the learning experience enjoyable. You might find it more valuable to spread the content of this Q&A as the subject matter needs to be broken down an explored to allow the children to develop a real connection and understanding to what is being taught. If you intend to play the 'current buns' game which is featured in this chapter, then this is a good opportunity to introduce the concept of what happens if you don't pay for things in the shops etc.

Teacher speaks to pupils

" *We are going to be learning about some important new words today. They are 'Rule of Law'. Let's say them together ... RULE OF LAW. Let's talk about what these words mean. 'Rule of law' is the rules that everyone who lives in this country must follow. They are like our school rules.*

Let us look at our school rules. Put your hand up if you know what our rules are. "

Have a discussion and list your rules. Give some examples and prompt the children if appropriate. Praise each child individually when they contribute to the discussion.

" *What do you think would happen if we did not have any school rules?* "

“ *Let us look at the rules in this country. How do they help to keep us safe?* ”

You can give examples, e.g. crossing the road, wearing a seat belt, etc.

“ *What do you think would happen if we did not have any rules in this country?* ”

You can give examples, e.g. stealing, or if no one queued when paying for their shopping etc.

“ *What would happen if everybody threw their rubbish on the floor instead of putting it in the bin?*

 Put your thumbs up if you think it is good to put your rubbish in the bin. ”

This is a good link to introducing the 'Keep Britain Tidy' game, detailed below.

“ *It is very important that we are kind to each other. You should never be unkind to anyone or speak to them in a way that might hurt their feelings.* ”

Talk about the variety of ways we can show kindness, including being kind to animals.

“ *Being a good friend is important. What should you do if you see someone showing unkind behaviour?* ”

Explain they should speak to a grown up, and consider introducing the word "bullying" if appropriate. Explain that you need to be strong in life (resilient) don't allow people to be unkind to you, etc.

“ *What words can we use to tell someone they have made us cross or sad?* ”

You can give examples, e.g. "no thank you", "not good", "no, stop, I don't like that", "your behaviour is making me very unhappy", "I'm going to tell a grown up" and so on.

    It is so nice when we are polite to each other. Let's make a list of polite words and talk about how we show good manners.

Write a list of key polite words and phrases to display in the classroom with your golden rules. Encourage the children to refer to them throughout the day.

    This is your classroom. It is very important to keep it tidy and not break the toys or tear the books. Sometimes though, we break things or hurt someone and we didn't mean to do it. This is called an 'accident'. What should you do if you hurt someone or break something by accident?

Emphasise that we all make mistakes and that we should never be afraid to tell the truth, because accidents happen to everyone.

    We are very lucky in this country. We have special people who work hard to look after us and keep us safe. Can you tell me who they are?

List parents, teachers, doctors, armed forces, shop assistants, etc.

    Children, I am so proud of you. You have all shown me how kind and clever you are. Well done for all your fantastic talking. Give yourselves a clap.

Activity – It's all at your Fingertips

The main learning intention of this activity is to develop the children's understanding of their uniqueness and how very special they are as individuals. The activity encourages the children to paint their hands and to notice that they have a unique imprint on their palms and fingertips. You can adapt it for older children to develop an awareness of how your fingerprints and DNA can link you to a crime scene (rule of law). However, in this instance, the message should remain positive. When the activity is completed, the hands can be used by the children as visual clues during circle time discussions and to vote with (democracy).

Step One

Prepare paint, paper, brushes, scissors, cello tape, straws or lolly sticks. This activity works well in one-to-one or small group situations, as the conversation is an important aspect of the activity.

Scenario

66 *We are going to do some hand printing. When the hand prints are dry, you can cut them out and stick them on lolly sticks or straws. You can choose. When we have circle time, you can use them instead of putting your hand up. What do you think of that idea then?*

Have a look at your hands. Can you see those lines? They are very special. On your fingertips, you have very tiny circles. Those circles are not like anyone else's, and no one in the world has the same circles on their fingertips as you. 99

Present this subject with a sense of enthusiasm. Convey how amazing you think it is.

" *Let's hold our hands out. Look at the lines on your palms. We all have them but it doesn't mean they are exactly the same. Wow I think this is so excellent, do you?* "

Encourage the children to compare their palms.

" *So you know we look at things about each other that are the same and things that are different? Well your finger prints are unique. Only you have those prints. How awesome you are!* "

You can expand on this by discussing similarities and differences that connect us or make us unique,

" *Well done everyone. Can you all help me clean up now please?* "

Game – Current Buns in the Baker's Shop

This game is a twist on the popular song and game 'Five Current Buns in a Baker's Shop'. The aims and learning intentions are for the children to develop an understanding of honesty, rules and consequences. The most important aspect of this game is for it to be a fun, fair, positive learning experience. The message of the game will have more relevance for the children if you speak to them about the rules of honesty, paying for items when you go to the shop, not stealing etc. prior to starting the game. The children I have introduced this game to appeared to be very excited about the prospect of going to prison or jail. If you think some children will get upset by the concept of prison just explain that it's "only a game" and let them be either a paying customer or a bun. Lyrics for the song can be found on the internet.

Preparing for the game

STEP ONE
Prepare either pretend money or a representation of money, for example, cut up pieces of paper.

STEP TWO
Prepare a cash register or a representation of one, for example, a box.

STEP THREE
Prepare a police officer's outfit or a representation of one, for example, a badge and or radio

STEP FOUR
Mark out two areas for the children to sit. One area should be the prison. The other area is for paying customers to sit with their buns.

Scenario

Divide the children into two groups sitting opposite each other.

" *We are going to play current buns.*

Some of you will be customers in a baker's shop. Some of you will be the buns the baker is selling. We are going to choose a police person and a shop person.

If you don't get a chance to be the police person or the shop person today, we will be playing the game again and I will make sure that everyone has a turn, so don't be upset if it's not your turn today.

We have been talking about making sure you pay for things when you go to the shops. We are going to pretend some of you haven't paid for your current buns so you will have to go to prison! Who wants to be the people who go to prison? "

Divide the customers into those with and those without money, and sing the current buns song.

When the non-paying customers pick their current bun, model what the police person has to say and then encourage them to say it.

" *Excuse me please, you haven't paid for that bun. Oh dear, not good, time to go to prison.* "

The police person will take the customer's hand and lead them to the designated prison area. They will sit with them while they wait for the next non-paying customer.

" *Oh dear, you must pay for things when you go to the shops or you will get into trouble.* "

Continue with this throughout the game, and praise the children for paying. Keep it fun.

" *Children, did you enjoy that game? Remember it's very important to pay for things when you go to the shops or you will get into trouble. Give yourselves a clap.* "

Activity – Speaker of the House

The learning intentions for this activity are for the children to show respect for others by listening to their view points, experiences and preferences. It aims to build the children's confidence, self esteem and resilience. Further more it will develop their communication,speech, attention and listening skills. This activity promotes some key principles from each of the four values. For example – Democracy – Having a say and listening to others view points and opinions – Rule of law – Having manners by not interrupting while someone else is speaking. Individual liberty and freedom for all – Being given choices, and encouragement to voice preferences, promoting childrens resilience particularly those who find it difficult to contribute to discussions and or have delayed speech and language development etc. Mutual respect and tolerance of those with different faiths and beliefs – Respect and tolerance for others thoughts, feelings, opinions and beliefs. Introduce the activity as "Speaker of the House" so children become familiar with this political terminology.

Scenario

Sit the children in a group. They can each hold their voting card. Either you or the children can ask questions, initiate a topic of conversation, or ask each child "what would you like to speak about?"

You should invite each child to contribute individually to the conversation. Whilst that child is speaking, they are the "Speaker of the House".

If appropriate, you could have a special chair and or a cloak for the person whose turn it is to speak. Alternatively, you could invite them to stand up.

When each child has finished speaking, they can put their voting card in the ballot box to signify that they have had a turn. Encourage the children to praise each other by clapping after each person has spoken.

Game – Keep Britain Tidy – Litter Bugs

The learning intentions for this game are to develop the children's understanding of the importance of "keeping Britain tidy". It is intended to be used in conjunction with discussions that encourage the children to look at the effects of litter on society and the environment.

The concept of the game is for the children to either race each other individually or as part of a team to see who can bag up rubbish e.g. empty cereal boxes etc. the fastest. The rubbish should be strategically placed either in the room or outdoor area to make it more competitive and fun. The winner or winners are the first ones to bag up all the rubbish.

You can make it more fun by including either wet or soggy materials to add a 'yucky' feel to the game. Most children will find this really funny. Additionally, you can give each item a point score, for example, a cereal box could be worth one point, and a sweet wrapper worth two points enabling you to link this into your mathematics planning. Encourage them to cheer each other on during the game and develop the children's resilience by prompting them not to give up, for example, if they have difficulty getting the rubbish in the bag.

First, discuss why keeping Britain tidy is important to establish context:

- Talk about the importance of putting rubbish in the bin. Give examples of how dirty the streets would be and how it affects others when people drop litter.

- Explain how rubbish and chemicals contaminate the environment. Use examples of the harm carrier bags and bottles do to animals.

- Talk about the beautiful parks, beaches and countryside that they might have visited, and how it should be respected.

- Discuss how throwing food on the floor will cause a smell, attracting rats and foxes. Extend this to include not letting dogs mess on the pavement.

- Encourage the children to put all their rubbish in the bin and to keep their school, home and outdoor places tidy.

Scenario

‟ *Children we are going to play a game today called "Litter Bugs". I'm going to give you a carrier bag each. You need to race each other to put all the rubbish into the bags. When all the rubbish is picked up, we will empty out the bags. The person with the most rubbish is the winner. First though, let me see if you have been listening to what I have been saying about why people need to put rubbish in the bin. Who can tell me why it is important not to throw wrappers or food on the floor?* ”

Observe whether the children are beginning to grasp what they have been taught. If this is their first introduction to the subject then focus on the key points listed on previous page. Remind them this is the "Rule of Law".

‟ *Well done children, good listening. Let's play the game!* ”

3

INDIVIDUAL LIBERTY
AND FREEDOM FOR ALL

Individual liberty and freedom for all

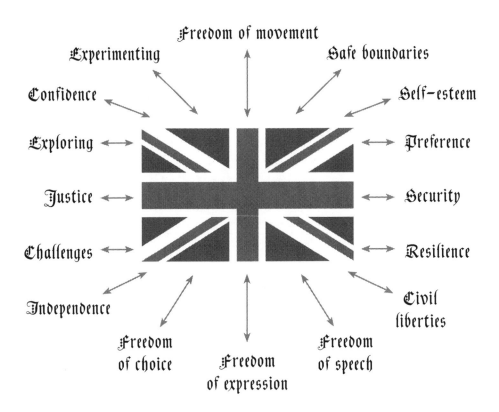

This section focuses on the right to express opinions, freedom of choice, being uninhibited to explore and challenge yourself within safe boundaries. It is about building resilience, persevering and never giving up. Encourage the children to speak openly about their experiences. Each individual child should be encouraged to talk about a preference, like or dislike to further develop their confidence and understanding of their right to free speech and civil liberties.

Teacher speaks to pupils

❝ *We are going to be learning about some very important words today. They are "individual liberty and freedom for all". Let us say them together ... INDIVIDUAL LIBERTY AND FREEDOM FOR ALL. Let us talk about what these words mean. They mean that people who live in this country and children who go to school do not have to be scared to talk about the things that are important to them. You are allowed to make choices, try new things, and explore different places. You are very lucky to be able to do this: some countries don't let people do the things they want to. It's very important to make sure that you're safe and not breaking any important rules though.* ❞

Remind the children of the "Rule of Law".

❝ *Let's talk about some of the things you have learned to do since you were babies.*

When we you were born you couldn't do anything for yourself. Now look at how much you have learned. ❞

Children love talking about when they were a baby. Talk about the fact that they needed a nappy and couldn't walk or talk etc. then encourage them to look at everything they have achieved. Use examples of learning to ride a bike or to get themselves dressed.

> " *If your Mums, Dads or whoever looks after you had not given you the chance to learn, you wouldn't be able to do anything on your own. You would still be like a baby.*
>
> *The people who care about you know that you have to do things for yourself, don't they? That's why children go to school, so you can learn to do things for yourself like read and write.* "

Use examples of learning to do things in school e.g. using scissors, writing, pouring your own drinks etc.

It is important to ask them if they found it difficult, talk about not giving up and to keep trying hard.

> " *You are very lucky that you have so many chances to learn and to become really good at things. You have to practise a lot, but that's how grown-ups learn to do things as well.* "

Give an example from your own experience of achieving something through perseverance.

> " *I would like you all to take turns to tell me something you really like doing.*
>
> *Now I would like you to tell me something you really don't like doing.* "

Ask the children if they ever refuse to do something. Try to expand on this so they get a sense of having some rights to speak out and have an opinion. Explain that some children in other countries are not allowed to go to school, explore or to have new and exciting experiences. Discuss how we are very fortunate in this country e.g. boys and girls have equal opportunities to learn.

" *What is your favourite toy?*

What is your favourite food?

How do you think you would feel if grown-ups never let you choose what you can play with? Put your hand up if you think that it would be unfair.

Do you think it is good to be able to try new activities? "

Talk about sometimes feeling a bit silly when you're learning to do something and/or the fact that they could hurt themselves when trying something new. Explain that it is sometimes part of learning how to do something well and safely.

" *What would you like to do when you grow up?*

If you want to do something but you find it hard to do, you have to believe in yourself, keep trying, never give up and remember how special you are.

Games are great fun. When you win, it can make you feel awesome. "

Discuss the games children like playing. Try to get a sense of if they understand about being competitive.

" *When you are playing a game and you don't win, how does it make you feel?*

There are important things to remember when you are learning. You need to enjoy being able to try new things and don't worry if you feel silly if you can't do it, it's ok. Keep trying and ask for help if you need it. Remember we talked about not being able to do things when you were a baby, now look at you! You are all amazing, well done. Give yourselves a clap. "

Activity – General election

The term "general election" can be used when you want the children to make collective choices and or input their ideas and opinions. The concept is to use this idea in conjunction with the ballot boxes and voting system. Initially, it might feel time consuming. However, when democratic systems are used consistently, they flow into your daily routine. Teaching British values needs to be fun, not monotonous. To begin with, try to use the ballot box once a day. Over time, learn what works best for you. The learning aims and intentions of this idea are to build children's independence, confidence vocabulary, and self-esteem, while developing their understanding of democracy and British culture.

Scenario

" *Good morning children. We are going to decide who are going to be the helpers today. Let's try a new way of choosing. Let's have a general election! Having a general election means we are all going to use our voting cards to make a decision. We are going to decide who the helpers are going to be today. This is exciting.* "

Select two small groups of potential helpers and ask the children to vote for which group of children they want to take on the role.

" *If you want Daniel, Maggie and Joshua to be the helpers, put your vote in the blue box. If you want Ailsa, Jessica and Kai to be the helpers, put your vote in the red box.* "

Further develop the children's understanding of democracy by reminding them that this is their choice and that their opinions matter.

" *We will now count the votes. Let's count them together.*

You have voted for Ailsa, Jessica and Kai to be the helpers today. Daniel, Maggie and Joshua will be the helpers tomorrow. Well done. You have just made a democratic decision. Give yourselves a clap. "

Game – Big Dinosaur, Little Dinosaur

The British Government is encouraging schools to re-introduce popular playground games. This is in light of the obesity epidemic amongst children. They want us to increase children's stamina and resilience – and what better way to do it than by playing games?

By introducing children to the principles of turn taking, respect, consideration and team work prior to playing games you can support the children's understanding of the social aspects of playing games. In addition to this, you can introduce new words, including "challenge", "win", "lose", "sportsmanship" etc. There are many opportunities to refer to the four values and principles during this game, further developing children's understanding of what they have already been taught on this subject. You could also use the voting system to offer them a choice of what characters they want to be if they don't want to be dinosaurs.

Big Dinosaur, Little Dinosaur is a gentle version of the 19th Century game 'British Bulldog'. The concept of the game is for a team of children to try to avoid being caught by an individual player. Once you have been caught, you have to help to catch the other children. The game is over when the last child has been caught. It has been adapted so that, instead of the children grabbing each other, they just need to touch the person. You can base the theme of the game around the children's interests – for example they could be lions instead of dinosaurs. Played with supervision, this is a fun way for children to get fit and build up their resilience.

Preparing for the game

STEP ONE
You will need a large area either outside or in a hall etc.

STEP TWO

Ask all the children to line up, with the exception of the child who is going to be the big dinosaur. He or she needs to stand in the middle of the playground. If you have a large class you might have to play two separate games.

Scenario

" *Children, the game we are going to play is called Big Dinosaur, Little Dinosaur.*

Does everyone want to be a dinosaur? You can be something else if you want. "

This is a good opportunity to refer to what the children have learnt about democracy using this scenario as an example. In addition to this you can tie in some of the principles of "Rule of Law" e.g. playing as a team, sportsmanship etc.

" *The children lining up are the little dinosaurs and the child in the middle is the big dinosaur. When the big dinosaur calls "come on little dinosaurs, I want to eat you all up", the little dinosaurs all say "You have to catch me first" and then run and try to touch the fence without being caught. If the big dinosaur touches you then, you have to help to catch your friends.*

The most important rules in this game are that you must not push or pull each other or someone might be hurt. You are only allowed to touch each other gently. Anyone who is too rough won't be allowed to play. Do you understand?

Right, good listening. Let's play the game. "

Praise the children during the game for persevering. When the game is finished, praise them for playing well.

Game – Egg and Spoon Race

This game has been included because it is quite difficult. The main learning intention is to develop the children's perseverance by encouraging them to keep going until they get to the finish line. It can be very frustrating when the egg keeps falling off the spoon, however it is a good way for the children to build resilience and strength of character. Encourage the children to see the funny side: humour can get you through most difficult challenges in life.

You can adapt this game by using different sized spoons or even a ladle. This will enable you to make it more or less difficult and provide opportunities for younger children and/or those with additional needs to join in and achieve success. Encourage the children to spur each other on and to clap at the end of each race.

Preparing for the game

STEP ONE
You will need to prepare appropriate sized spoons, depending on each child's stage of development, and plastic eggs, small balls or egg shaped objects – anything that can balance in a spoon.

You can race the children against each other either in groups of two or more depending on class size and or space

Scenario

❝ *Children, we are going to have a race. It's called an egg and spoon race. You will need to balance an egg on a spoon and race each other without dropping it. It's quite hard to do, but if the egg drops on the floor you just pick it up and keep going until you get to the end.*

The rules are that you must not hold the egg on the spoon: you must balance it. If you hold it on, then it's cheating, which is not good behaviour. Is cheating good behaviour? ❞

Explain why cheating isn't fair on their friends, that they won't learn to do something properly if they give up or win by cheating. Divide the children into groups or teams and start playing.

4

MUTUAL RESPECT AND
TOLERANCE OF THOSE
WITH DIFFERENT
FAITHS AND BELIEFS

Mutual Respect and Tolerance of Those with Different Faiths and Beliefs

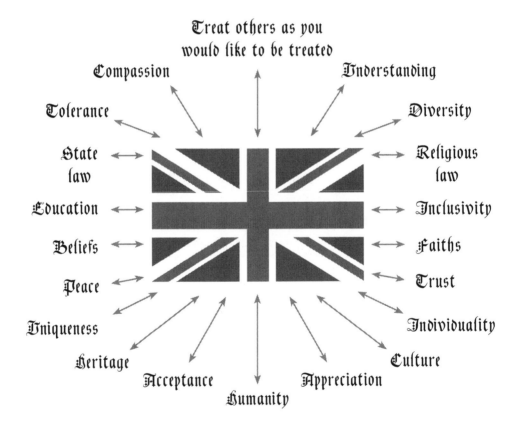

This section will focus on creating an ethos of inclusivity, tolerance, appreciation and consideration of others. The children should be encouraged to talk about things they like doing with their families, including holidays, recreational past times and going to places of worship. Encourage the children to identify similarities and differences that connect us or make us unique. Look at cultural and historical land marks to develop an understanding of heritage. The children should be encouraged to clap at the end of the session to show appreciation of each other's experiences, uniqueness and diversity.

Teacher speaks to pupils

We are going to be learning about some special words today. They are mutual respect and tolerance. Let us say them together … MUTUAL RESPECT AND TOLERANCE. Let's look at what these words mean.

Mutual respect is when we value each other and treat each other with kindness and appreciation. Tolerance is when you accept that people are different. You might not like things about another person, and some things they do might make you cross. You might not believe in the same things they believe in. Tolerance is when you can understand and accept that everyone in this world has things about them that are the same, and things about them that are very different. It doesn't matter if you are different, we are all special.

Call two children up, making sure that they are different from each other e.g. boy, girl, hair and skin colour etc. This is to encourage children to identify the similarities and differences that connect us and or make us unique.

❝ *Do you think we all look the same? Let's look at things about us that are the same.* ❞

Use the children as examples. Talk about us all having a heart, eyes, noses, etc.

❝ *Let's talk about ways we are different.* ❞

Mention we do not always have the same hair or skin colour. Include people with disabilities in the discussion e.g. they might be in a wheelchair or unable to see properly etc. Emphasise the importance of people being special rather than different.

❝ *Do you think it is ok to be unkind to someone just because they are not like you?*

If I came into school and I had been in an accident that made my face look a bit scary, would you still like me or would you be horrible to me?

I like all of you because of your lovely behaviour and kindness. If you looked different, I would still like you.

Let us talk about ways we show kindness (mutual respect) and understanding (tolerance) for each other in our classroom.

The way we speak to each other is very important. It isn't nice to show unkind behaviour or use unkind words. Can you think of a time when someone has made you cross or angry? ❞

Give examples of the way we speak to each other and/or appropriate ways of behaving towards someone who has upset us. Give examples of the types of vocabulary they should use.

❝ *Shall we take turns to talk about what we do when we are not in school/nursery?* ❞

Encourage the children to discuss their family outings and extended families. Get an insight into their cultural back grounds. Explain that not all families are the same.

> *We are very lucky to live in this country. Do you know the name of this country? Lots of people who live in this country were not born here, but it is their home.*

Prompt children to comment on their cultural background, for example, does anyone speak a different language, etc.

> *Do you know any famous places in London?*

Link this to the famous landmarks 'What's Gone Missing' game. This can extend to landmarks outside London and abroad.

> *Has anyone heard of the Royal Family? Let us look at members of the Royal Family.*

Link this to the Royal family "Who's Gone Missing" game. Show the children the pictures if you have them ready.

> *Well done children, it's been so lovely to listen to you all. Give yourselves a big clap for being so special.*

Activity – I Believe

The learning intentions for this activity are for the children to begin to develop an understanding, acceptance and or tolerance of other beliefs. It is an introduction to the concept of everyone being entitled to have their own opinions as to what or who they believe in. The aim is to be able to expand on this as they get older to include more sensitive issues regarding different religious beliefs and the negative behaviour of some people in society. The children will be asked to draw pictures of what they believe in. You can then make an album featuring their work. Children tend to say they believe in super heroes and princesses … this is fine let them draw what they want.

Scenario

66 *Children, let's talk about the different things you believe in. When I was little and my tooth came out, I used to put it under my pillow for the tooth fairy. Do any of you believe in the tooth fairy?*

Let's go around the class to see what everyone believes in. 99

Encourage the children to recall any past experiences or thoughts about what they believe in.

66 *Now that I'm a grown up, I believe in different things. I believe it is very important to believe in yourself and to never give up. Some people believe in God and baby Jesus and some people don't. Some people believe in Father Christmas and some people don't. Some people believe in Allah and some people don't.*

Did you know that some people are unkind to other people just because they don't believe in the same things? This is not good behaviour, it's silly behaviour.

Do we want to have that behaviour in our school or in our country? 99

" *I have a good idea: you can write about something you believe in and draw a picture of it. We can make a special book and put all your pictures in the book so we can all look at them. Do you think that sounds like a good idea?* "

If the children can't write yet, encourage them to mark make and to relay back what they have drawn. When you make the book, leave it so that the children can access it and discuss each other's beliefs.

" *Give yourselves a clap.* "

Activity – All About Me

The concept of this activity is for the children to make photo albums with pictures of their family etc in them. The learning intentions are for the children to share experiences and to develop an understanding of each other's cultural backgrounds and diversity. The books should be easily accessible and the children encouraged to share their albums and experiences with their peers. You can expand on this by looking at each child's album during a group circle time and encourage the children to stand up individually and talk through their album.

You will need to buy or make books (albums), and encourage the children and parents/carers to bring in pictures from home. This will help to develop a good partnership between home, nursery and or school. Explain the concept to parents.

Game – Who's Gone Missing?

The main learning intentions for this game are for the children to develop an interest in and understanding of another significant part of our British culture and heritage. It aims to develop the children's recognition of members of the Royal Family.

This is a twist on the popular 'Kym's' game. The concept of the game is for the children to be able to tell you which picture of one of the members of the Royal Family has gone missing. I have found the concept of this game is excellent for teaching the children anything from healthy eating, rhyming words to recognising national flags, you can try any subject.

STEP ONE

You will need to laminate at least 8 pictures of members of the Royal Family, particularly Prince Williams's family as children love babies. Whilst selecting pictures, it is advantageous to pick ones of distinct individuals, as children are unlikely at this point to be able to recognise the Royal Family by name. However, they might be able to recall key characteristics, such as gender, age and hair colour.

STEP TWO

You will need a large cloth or form of cover, so you can hide the pictures from view.

Scenaio

Children sit on the carpet. You sit a suitable distance opposite from them so they are not tempted to touch the pictures.

Explain to the children.

" *We are going to play a game.* "

Hold up all the pictures individually introducing each one, for example, "This is a picture of the Queen".

Select three of the key members of the family, laying them face up on the carpet in front of you.

Point to each picture, name them individually, and tell the children:

> " *I want you to hide your eyes. I am going to take one picture away, and then you have to tell me which picture has gone missing. If you peep it's cheating. Remember what we have been learning about the 'Rule of Law'.* "

Encourage the children to hide their eyes while you cover the pictures, as this adds to the excitement. Take a picture away, hiding it under the cover.

> " *You can open your eyes now. What picture has gone missing?* "

Until the children recognise the people, they are going to need prompting.

Encourage the children to name the picture that you have removed, and point to the remaining two pictures on the carpet, naming them individually to develop their recognition.

> " *If you don't know who has gone missing, I can give you a clue ...* "

Give the children clues, reveal the picture when appropriate. The more familiar they become, the more pictures you can introduce to make the game more challenging.

> " *Well done children, you used your brains. Very good looking and listening, give yourselves a clap.* "

Game – What's Gone Missing?

You can use the same concept as "Who's Gone Missing" using famous British landmarks. You might want to expand on this by encouraging the children to research famous landmarks from around the world, particularly if they are from a different cultural background. This will support you in providing an ethos of inclusivity and respect for cultural diversity and heritage.

Examples of famous British landmarks include

Tower Bridge	The Angel of the North
Houses of Parliament	Ben Nevis
Buckingham Palace	Globe Theatre
St. Paul's Cathedral	Edinburgh Castle
Stonehenge	The London Eye
Windsor Castle	Loch Ness
Westminster Abbey	

Examples famous landmarks from around the world include

The Statue of Liberty in the USA	Niagara Falls in Canada
The Eiffel Tower in France	Mount Everest in Nepal
The Great Wall of China	The Grand Canyon in the USA
The Taj Mahal in India	The Coliseum in Italy
The Leaning Tower of Pisa in Italy	St Basil's Cathedral in Russia

ADDITIONAL
RESOURCES

Make learning 'the principles' more engaging

Having a democratic process in the classroom where you listen to children's ideas and viewpoints, can support you in making your teaching and their learning more interesting and fun. Children tend to be more engaged when they are actively taking part. You can encourage them to participate by, for example, contributing their work to wall displays, asking them to bring in objects, pictures, memorabilia, and cultural artefacts from home etc. The games and activities in this book have worked really well in my setting because they are very visual and require the children's impute, for example, when making and using the 'Ballot boxes'. From my experience, props used confidently and skilfully can support you in teaching aspects of the British values principles. Take for example the story of "Goldilocks and the Three Bears". If you're learning intentions are to teach the children right from wrong (Rule of law) and or 'stranger danger', then you could ask them, "Should you go into a stranger's house, was it good that Goldilocks ate (stole) baby bears porridge and broke the chair?" and so on. You could relate the story of the "Ugly Duckling" or "The Hunch back of Notre Dame" to "Mutual Respect and Tolerance" by discussing how those characters were treated unkindly (faced discrimination) because they were different or considered ugly etc.

Listed in the resources section is a selection of familiar topics that will work well in supporting your teaching of the values. However, if you are organised in the vocabulary you are going to use, how the learning intentions are going to be met, and use some skilful analogies, you can probably incorporate them to some extent into any topic. For example, when teaching about wild animals – lions

- "Democracy" Do they have a democracy, are all the Pride involved in the decision making process or is it a dictatorship, how do they settle disputes and or disagreements?

- "Rule of law" Do they have rules and social boundaries, are they kind, supportive and loving towards each other?

- "Individual liberty and freedom for all" Are the cubs given choices, opportunities to explore their environment and to learn new skills, are they encouraged to build their resilience and to not 'give up'?

- "Mutual respect and tolerance" Do they have a family structure, promote inclusivity and gender equality, how do they treat those in the Pride who are born with a disability or who are weak and or wounded, do they show tolerance towards other animals, those who are different from them?

I would suggest that if you are not already doing so, make a 'British values' key and initial your planning. Show how you are incorporating the values and principles into different subjects, even if you are just using some key words and or phrases etc. Be very clear in your own mind of what the learning intentions are in relation to the values, particularly when planning topics. This will give you some supporting evidence to prove to Ofsted you are actively teaching them.

Ultimately, your qualities and attitude towards teaching the values are going to be what motivates and influences the children to engage in learning. Concepts and words that children don't understand need to have vibrancy for them to want to learn their meaning, so lots of expression is needed. Humour is powerful stratagem to gain children's attention. If you combine firm boundaries with having fun, then there is more chance of getting the children to pay attention when you want them to listen and learn. This is because they ... wait for it ... like you and want you to like them in return. Laughter helps to build relationships and genuine warmth. The children will feel a connection to you and value your approval ... give it a try!

Suggested Topics for Teaching 'the Principles'

The World Around Us	Animals in their Natural Habitats
Occupations	Seasons
People and Places	Celebrations
Similarities and Differences	Holidays
The Five Senses	Starting School
Feelings and Emotions	Famous People
Healthy Eating	Famous Landmarks
Dental Health and Hygiene	The Royal Family
The Human Body and How We Evolve	Where Does Our Food Come From?
Pets and Caring for Animals	Lifecycles
Stone Age Britain	The Tudors
Traditional British and multicultural food	National Costumes

Historic celebrations

As a nation we recognise and embrace a diverse range of religious and cultural celebrations. Listed below are a selection of 'special days' that could be seen as being "typically British", they might not all have originated in this country however they are very much part of our culture. It is important to add that many of these examples are recognised and celebrated around the world. Included are a variety of themed activities traditionally associated with celebrating these events.

The Queens Birthday – June

The Queen was born in 1926. The country celebrates her 'official birthday' in June. This dates back to 1748.

Dressing up theme day	Bunting
English flag	Street party
Crowns	Afternoon tea and scones with small world tea set

St David's Day – 1ˢᵗ March

St David is the Patron saint of Wales – he was a renowned teacher and ascetic. Celebrations date back to the 18th century.

Daffodil handprints	Dragon face junk modelling
Face painting	St David's Day shields
Daffodil shaped biscuits	

St Patricks Day – 17th March

The Feast of Saint Patrick celebrates the arrival of Christianity in Ireland. It dates back to 17th century.

4 leaf clover junk models	Face painting
4 leaf clover cupcakes	St Patrick's day shape printing with green paint and peppers
Leprechaun hats/Blarney stones	

Resurrection Sunday – March-April

The celebration of Christ's resurrection is more commonly referred to as Easter Sunday. Honouring this event dates back to the mid-2nd century.

Easter egg hunt	Hot cross bun tea party
Easter bonnet parade	Cards
Rice Krispy bird nest cakes	Decorating eggs

Mothering Sunday – March-April

This is a celebration which began with honouring the 'Mother church'. It evolved overtime to become a celebration to honour Mothers and mother figures. It started to become Commercial in the 1930's.

Tissue paper flowers	Cakes
Cards	Jewellery
Certificates	Children's hand/foot prints clay
Junk model picture frames	moulds/paint etc

St George's Day – 23th April

St George's Day is the feast day of St George. He became revered by the English. As legend has it, he fought beside the English in the 'Crusades' and 'Hundred-years' war'. References to honouring him date back to the ninth century.

Flags	Castle role play
Junk/clay model dragons/castles	St George and the dragon pictures
Masks/swords	

Father's Day – Third week in June

This is a celebration to honour fathers and father figures which dates back to 1910.

Tie cards	Certificates
Junk model cars	Paper cup pen holder
Trophies/medals	Initialled biscuits

Notting Hill Carnival – August

Notting Hill Carnival is a street festival that attracts people from around the world. It dates back to 1966.

Masks	Streamers
Cultural food street party (involve parents)	Multi-Cultural music/instruments/dance
Face painting	Making musical instruments

Harvest Festival – September

This celebration is to give thanks for a good crop or harvest. It dates back to Pagan times.

Thank you cards	Mud cakes/play
Farming pictures	Fruit and vegetable collage/printing

Guy Fawkes Night – November 5th

This day celebrates the failure of Guy Fawkes to blow up the Houses of Parliament. It has evolved from the '5th of November Act' which dates back to 1605.

Pictures of fireworks/bonfires	Lemonade and Mentos fountain
Make a guy	Junk model rockets/Catherine wheels etc

Remembrance Day – November

Remembrance Day – which is sometimes referred to as Poppy Day – has been held since the end of the First World War in 1918. It is marked by a two-minute silence to remember the members of the armed forces who died in the line of duty. It is related to Armistice Day, Veterans Day, Memorial Day and Anzac Day.

Poppy pictures/wreaths	Afternoon tea/street party
Flags	Nostalgic music
Bottle top medals	Buntings

St Andrew's Day – 30ᵗʰ November

It is documented that St Andrew was with Jesus at the Last Supper. He became the Patron Saint of Scotland in 1320. The feast day of St Andrew dates back to 1034.

Cards	Flags
Tartan effect printing and crafts	St Andrew's Day place mats

Christmas Day – 25ᵗʰ December

Christmas Day commemorates the birth of Jesus Christ. It dates back to Roman times.

Grotto/ role play	Nativity
Wrapping presents	Carol songs
Christmas cards	Tree decorations etc

Let's have a 'Good Old Fashioned Singsong'

Children love songs and rhymes. Although it is beneficial for children's learning to be repetitive, it can become monotonous to sing the same tunes over and over. As with children's games, we forget what an amazing variety of songs and rhymes there are. They are a huge part of British heritage and bridge the generation gap between the young and the old. The rhymes below are all British and written in the 18th and 19th Centuries. They have stood the test of time proving that … Britain really did have talent! You can link these to your literacy and 'British values' planning

Pattacake, Pattacake (1698)	Humpty Dumpty (1797)
Little Jack Horner (1725)	Bobby Shafto's Gone to Sea (1805)
London Bridge is Falling Down (1744)	Little Bo Peep (1805)
Mary, Mary Quite Contrary (1744)	Little Miss Muffet (1805)
Jack and Jill (1765)	Twinkle, Twinkle Little Star (1806)
Seesaw Margery Daw (1765)	Jack be Nimble (1815)
Hot Cross Buns (1797)	Doctor Foster (1844)
Round the Mulberry bush (1850)	Ring of Roses (1881)

Those were the days!

Teaching children aspects of our British heritage can be basic, enjoyable and fun. Songs, rhymes, familiar stories and games old and new are already being taught. We do not have to introduce new complicated concepts just preserve some old traditions. We forget how many games are out there that have given pleasure to children for centuries. You can use the ballot box so children can vote on which game they want to play, promoting individual liberty and freedom for all and democracy.

Some 'oldies but goodies' include:

Duck, Duck, Goose	Musical Statues
Current Buns	Musical Chairs
Simon Says	Musical Bumps
Cops and Robbers	Hoopla
British Bulldog	Dodgeball
Follow the Leader	Kerbsey
London Bridge	Football
Skipping	Hopscotch
Egg and Spoon Race	Ring of Roses
Stuck in the Mud	Piggy in the Middle
Snakes and ladders	Snap

If in Doubt, Get a Book Out

As the saying goes 'you can't beat a good book', especially if you want to get an important message across to children in a visual, fun and interesting way. The department for education have listed a selection of books that could be used to support the teaching of British values. I have listed additional titles under sub headings related to different areas of S.M.S.D and British values principles. The content is suitable for children Preschool to Key Stage 2.

Confidence and self esteem
I Like Myself *by Karen Beaumont and David Catrow*
Giraffes can't Dance *by Giles Andreae*

Kindness
The Lion and the Mouse *by Jerry Pinkney*
How do Dinosaurs play with their friends *by Jane Yolan*

Compassion and caring
The Teddy Bear by David Mcphail
A Sick Day for Amos McGee *by Philip Stead*

Honesty
The Boy who Cried Big Foot *by Scot Magoon*
Princess K.I.M and the Lie That Grew *by Maryanne Cocco Leffler*

Manners
Time to say Please *by Mo Wilems*
Mind your Manners B.B.Wolf *by Judy Sierra*

Gratitude and thankfulness
An Awesome Book of Thanks *by Dallas Clayton*
There's a flower at the tip of my nose smelling me *by Alice Walker*

Generosity and sharing

My friend Fred *by Hiawyn Oram*

The mine-o-Saur *by Sudipta Quallen*

Service and helping others

The Mitten tree *by Candice Christiansen*

How to heal a broken wing *by Bob Graham*

Diversity and tolerance

The skin you live in *by Michael Tyler and David Csicsko*

OK to be different *by Todd Parr*

Individuality

Leon the Chameleon *by Melanie Watt*

Ella Sarah gets dressed *by Margaret Chodos Irvine*

Judging on appearances

Big Al *by Andrew Clements*

Stand tall *by Molly Lou Melon and Patty Lovell*

Open mindedness

Duck! Rabbit! *by Amy Krause*

Having courage

A little book about taking a leap *by Marian Van Lieshout*

The terrible plot *by Ursula Dubosarsky*

Creative thinking

Westlanda *by Paul Fleischman*

Not a box *by Antoinette Poutis*

Elephants can paint too *by Katya Arnold*

Rule of Law – Table Manners

One of the 'British values' principles is to teach children table manners. Historically, children were expected to sit up straight at the table, hands on laps, not speaking, while waiting for everyone to be served. Furthermore, they were required to always say please/thankyou, to use a knife and fork correctly (never your fingers) and a spoon and fork when eating desert. Slopping, belching, fidgeting and getting down from the table without permission were all big 'no, no's. Meal times should be a pleasant experience, however if you are teaching 'British values' then sitting at the table, being polite, chewing with your mouth closed and being encourage to use cutlery properly, is arguably a 'must'.

In relation to what Ofsted inspectors want to see … then in my experience, this is a grey area. Be mindful that the children are not waiting too long to eat … another big 'no, no'. If you have particularly young children in your setting, then make sure your expectations are realistic, particularly in relation to how long the children are expected to sit at the table, keeping their hands on laps and when using cutlery and so on. Below is a fun song that can support you in teaching this subject.

Lunch is coming: Tune Frere Jacques – You can replace the word 'lunch' with snack and or tea

<blockquote>
Lunch is coming, lunch is coming!
Are we ready, are we ready!
Fingers off the table, fingers off the table!
Hands on your laps, hands on your laps!
Please and thank you, please and thank you!
We must say, we must say!
When we're given something, when we're given something!
Every day, every day.
</blockquote>

British "Grub"

It's interesting when trying to define what we 'now days' consider to be 'typically British' food. As a nation we have a love of what are considered 'multicultural foods' which is reflected in our vast array of restaurants, take-a-way establishments and in Supermarkets. The meal 'Fish and chips' was first served in this country in 1858, however the first recorded Indian restaurant in this country was in 1809. Figures show that Indian cuisine it is currently the most popular in Britain, therefore, you could argue that it is equally a part our heritage as fish and chips ... Interesting! This certainly makes our history of food appear a bit more exciting, as we still have a reputation for serving 'bland, stodgy food' (Sorry ... Not you Jamie Oliver). It may be important to add that we were doing quite well up until the first and second world wars, which resulted in severe rationing and changed the face of the nation's diet. This book includes references to aspects of our culture that are perceived to be 'Very British' I've listed below some examples of this. Tastes in food change as cultures evolve, these examples may not be as popular now, however they are part of our heritage.

Suggested topics – "British and cultural foods from around the world", "Healthy eating":

Roast beef and Yorkshire pudding	Fish pie
Fish and chips	Lancashire hot pot
Bubble and squeak	Pie-mash and liquor
Steamed steak and kidney pudding	Cornish pasties
Beef stew and dumplings	Ploughman's lunch
Shepherd's pie	Black pudding
Poultry based casseroles	Haggis (Scottish)
Bangers (sausages) and mash	Welsh rarebit
Toad-in-the-hole	Dumplings
	Full English breakfast 'Fry up'

Porridge

Crumpets

Tea and toast

Cheddar cheese (we produce over 400 varieties of cheese in this country)

Sweet dishes include

Apple Crumble

Spotted dick and custard

Chelsea bun

Rice pudding

Semolina

Eton mess

Bread and butter pudding

Trifle

Victoria sponge

Scones/ Rock cake

Shortbread

Jelly and ice cream

Mince pies

Christmas pudding

Jam tarts

Stewed rhubarb/fruit and custard

Bread pudding

Jams, preserves and chutneys

Clotted cream

Battenberg cake

Chelsea bun

Eton mess

BRITISH NATIONAL ANTHEM

The British National Anthem is called 'God save the Queen'. It became known as the National Anthem from the beginning of the nineteenth century, however it originated as a patriotic song performed in 1745. The National Anthem is generally performed on official occasions; you might want to introduce it to the children to be sung on special occasions, for example if you have a graduation ceremony.

God save our gracious Queen!
Long live our noble Queen
God save the Queen!
Send her victorious,
Happy and glorious,
Long to reign over us,
God save the Queen

The British National Anthem represents the whole of the United Kingdom. However, Scotland and Wales have other songs they sing particularly when they play against England in sport events.

Wales – Hen Wlad Fy Nhadau (Land of My Fathers)

Scotland – Flower of Scotland and Scotland the Brave

CONCLUSION

I hope you feel inspired to use some of the ideas in this book. It will take a bit of time, consistency and enthusiasm to implement some of the activities and games. However, the children will enjoy it and you will have some tangible evidence to show that you have been teaching the British values and principles. Don't be put off by introducing complex words. I just remind myself that we have children in our setting who are four years old and can communicate well in three different languages ... Its amazing! ... keep an open mind

21273564R00049

Printed in Poland
by Amazon Fulfillment
Poland Sp. z o.o., Wrocław